SUPERNATURAL SCIENCE

VAMPIRE
INVESTIGATORS

BY
MADELINE TYLER

Gareth Stevens
PUBLISHING

Please visit our website, www.garethstevens.com. For a free color catalog of all our high-quality books, call toll free 1-800-542-2595 or fax 1-877-542-2596.

Cataloging-in-Publication Data

Names: Tyler, Madeline.
Title: Vampire investigators / Madeline Tyler.
Description: New York : Gareth Stevens Publishing, 2020. | Series: Supernatural science
| Includes glossary and index.
Identifiers: ISBN 9781538253090 (pbk.) | ISBN 9781538253106 (library bound) | ISBN 9781538254141 (6 pk)
Subjects: LCSH: Vampires–Juvenile literature.
Classification: LCC BF1556.T95 2020 | DDC 398'.45–dc23

First Edition

Published in 2020 by
Gareth Stevens Publishing
111 East 14th Street, Suite 349
New York, NY 10003

Copyright © 2019 Booklife Publishing
This edition is published by arrangement with Booklife Publishing

Written by: Madeline Tyler
Edited by: John Wood
Designed by: Drue Rintoul

All images are courtesy of Shutterstock.com, unless otherwise specified. With thanks to Getty Images, Thinkstock Photo and iStockphoto. Front Cover – Fer Gregory. 2 – Yuriy Mazur. 4&5 – Vasilyev Alexandr, berrydog, Vita Fortuna, Ursatii. 6&7 – u3d, marymyyr. 8&9 – pedrosala, Alexander Raths. 10&11 – guteksk7, Ursatii, Olha Bocharova, secondcorner. 12&13 – sripfoto, hrui, Artram, DR-images, nikkytok. 14&15 – Erik D, Sandratsky Dmitriy, Daboost, Karramba Production, andrea crisante, Lina_Lisichka, stuar, Hayati Kayhan, Third of november. 16&17 – Morphius Film, By Maxrossomachin [CC BY-SA 3.0 (https://creativecommons.org/licenses/by-sa/3.0) or GFDL (http://www. gnu.org/copyleft/fdl.html)], from Wikimedia Commons. 18&19 – solarseven , Chromatika Multimedia snc, plampy, mrfotos, Andrei Mayatnik. 20&21 – stuar, Hayati Kayhan, cobalt88, Olga Popova, Alexander_P, AFANASEV IVAN. 22&23 – Volonoff, Lev Kropotov, DiegoMariottini, Alexander Lukatskiy, stellamc. 24&25 – Laurinson Crusoe, Yulduz, aradaphotography. 26&27 – SOMKKU, Andrey Eremin, Andrey_Kuzmin, Valentyn Volkov, Stock Vector, 279photo Studio, DenisMArt, yurchello108. 28&29 – canbedone, mike tutt photography, Michael Rosskothen. 30 – Fer Gregory.

Printed in the United States of America

CPSIA compliance information: Batch #CW20GS: For further information contact Gareth Stevens, New York, New York at 1-800-542-2595.

CONTENTS

WORDS THAT LOOK LIKE THIS ARE EXPLAINED IN THE GLOSSARY ON PAGE 31.

What Are Vampires, Anyway?

Do you know anyone who's afraid to leave the house during the day? Do they avoid sunlight at all costs? Do they only step outside when it's particularly cloudy, or well after the sun has gone down? Their skin is probably so pale that it's almost TRANSPARENT. Now, this isn't strange on its own – in fact, many people try to stay out of the sunlight because they're worried that they will get burned. However, if this person also has sharp fangs, cold skin, and a taste for blood, then there's something you should know...

VAMPIRES ARE BELIEVED TO HAVE RED EYES, FANGS, AND COLD, PALE SKIN. THEY ARE ALSO SAID TO FEED ON HUMAN BLOOD BY BITING THEIR VICTIMS ON THE NECK.

Some people believe that vampires have been living alongside us for CENTURIES. According to vampire investigators, they hide in the shadows and wait until it's dark before they PREY on their victims. They are said to be very INTELLIGENT and very hard to spot. This makes it hard for people to prove that vampires exist.

Some people believe that vampires are real, while other people think that they only exist in scary films and spooky stories. Whether you believe in vampires or not, a good vampire investigator always tries their best to solve the mystery and uncover the truth. It will be your job to track the clues, follow any LEADS, and collect the evidence.

DO YOU HAVE SOMEONE IN MIND THAT YOU THINK COULD BE A VAMPIRE? KEEP A CLOSE EYE ON THEM AND DON'T LET THEM OUT OF YOUR SIGHT!

If you want to become a real vampire investigator, then pay close attention as you read this book. Investigating vampires is no easy task. It takes skill, bravery, and lots of research. There's plenty of information out there about vampires – you just need to know where to look. If you're feeling brave and you're ready to start your supernatural journey, turn the page and see what's out there...

Language of a
Vampire Investigator

So, you've decided that you definitely want to be a real-life vampire investigator. You'll be carrying out lots of scientific investigations, so you'll need to learn the right words to use. Many of these words will be quite complicated and may not seem to make much sense at first, but don't worry – they're not that difficult to understand!

ACCURATE:
careful and free from mistakes

ANALYZE:
to examine something carefully in order to explain and understand

AVERAGE:
the typical amount or most central number of a range of numbers

CONTROL:
things that don't change, which can then be compared against things that do

CONTROL VARIABLES:
the parts of an experiment that are kept the same

DEPENDENT VARIABLES:
the parts of an experiment that you measure

ESTIMATE:
to make a careful guess about something

EVIDENCE:
something that gives proof and can be used to give reason to believe in something

FAIR:
playing by the rules, or treating everything and everyone equally

INDEPENDENT VARIABLE:
the part of an experiment that you change

MEAN:
the number you get when you add a list
of numbers up and divide it by how many
numbers there are in the list, giving you
the average number

MEDIAN:
the number in the middle of a list of numbers
when the numbers are ordered from lowest to
highest or from highest to lowest

MODE:
the number that appears the most often when
a list of numbers is ordered from lowest to
highest or highest to lowest

OBSERVATIONS:
things that you can see or notice from your
experiment that you can then record

PLOT:
to mark data points on a graph

PRECISE:
exact, specific, and accurate

PREDICTIONS:
guesses of what will happen in the future

RANGE:
the difference between the biggest and smallest
number. You can find the range by taking the
smallest number away from the biggest number

RELIABLE:
can be trusted

DON'T PANIC
IF YOU FIND A WORD
IN THIS BOOK THAT YOU'RE
NOT SURE OF. JUST FLICK BACK
TO THIS PAGE TO REMIND
YOURSELF OF WHAT
IT MEANS.

It's Time to Investigate!

Working Scientifically

A big part of being a vampire investigator is working scientifically. You may know some vampire basics and a handful of important scientific words, but that doesn't mean that you can just head out into the world in search of bloodsucking vampires. First, you need to know how to carry out some scientific investigations. You'll need to work like a true scientist, being as accurate and as precise as possible, no matter how scared you might be. If your results are reliable, then people will be more likely to take your research seriously and trust your investigations.

Science is all about asking lots of questions. These questions help scientists to gather accurate information from their investigations. Here are some questions to ask yourself during your own investigations:

- What is it that I'm trying to find out?
- Do I have the right equipment?
- Will changing different things in my investigation make it fairer?
- What can I do to make my measurements more accurate and precise?

Have you **IDENTIFIED** what you're trying to find out? As soon as you've decided, you can start to prepare all the other parts of your investigation. Are you tracking down where a vampire might live or are you trying to tempt them out with some tasty human blood? Perhaps you're secretly adding garlic to all of your family's meals and studying how everyone reacts? As soon as you have a plan for your investigation, you can begin to collect your equipment, decide on your variables, and make a prediction.

Remember, although being brave is important, it's only part of your mission as a vampire investigator. You also need to learn how to carry out experiments like a real scientist. Do you think you can do it?

Predictions and Results

When your investigation is all set up, one of the first things you'll need to do is make a prediction. A prediction, or an estimate, is a bit like a very well-thought-out guess. It could be based on something that you already know, or maybe the results from a previous experiment. Predictions are very important because they make us really think about our investigation and what we think the outcome will be.

You should always think about the different things that could affect your investigation. How would changing the different variables in your experiment change your results? Are there some things that you could change to make it fairer?

It's always a good idea to write down your prediction in a notepad. This will help you to remember it and also give you something to think about when you carry out your investigation.

As well as noting down your predictions, it's also important to record your results. When the experiment is over, you'll need to analyze your findings and see how similar or different they are to your predictions. It doesn't matter if your investigation didn't go the way you were expecting – you can still learn a lot!

If you think that something went wrong, you can always repeat your investigation. You can do this as many times as you like. You can then find the mode, median, mean, and range of your results. Finding the mean of all of your repeated investigations will tell you what your average result is.

Plotting your results on a graph can make them easier to understand and study. This graph could be a line graph, a bar chart, or a pie chart. Make sure you know which graph suits your results best. What information can you gather from this line graph?

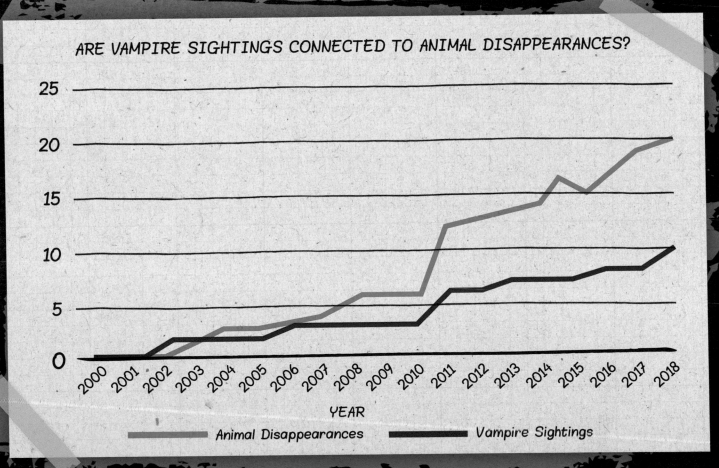

ARE VAMPIRE SIGHTINGS CONNECTED TO ANIMAL DISAPPEARANCES?

YEAR

Animal Disappearances — Vampire Sightings

THIS LINE GRAPH SHOWS THE NUMBER OF ANIMAL DISAPPEARANCES COMPARED WITH VAMPIRE SIGHTINGS OVER 18 YEARS. CAN YOU SEE ANY CONNECTION?

Investigation 1: Out in the Dark

Do you think you know everything there is to know about vampires? If you want to become a top vampire investigator, then you'll need to brush up on your vampire basics before you're ready to go out into the wild.

Vampires have appeared in stories across the world for hundreds of years. From the vrykolakas of Greece to the Indian Brahmaparusha, they are everywhere. Brahmaparusha is said to hang upside down from trees, just like a bat, and suck the blood of its victims. Vrykolakas are bloodsucking monsters, too. They are believed to drink so much blood that their skin turns red!

In almost every vampire story that exists, vampires only come out at night. As no one has ever been able to confirm whether or not vampires are real, it's difficult to know exactly why this might be. Does the sunlight burn their skin and set them on fire? Or do they just prefer the darkness? No one knows.

Some vampire investigators have suggested that, if vampires do exist, perhaps they are **NOCTURNAL** like bats. Their skin and eyes could be so used to the darkness that it would be painful to go outside in the sunlight. They would be blinded by the bright light and their skin would burn very easily. There's no way that they would risk going outside in the bright daylight.

IF VAMPIRES ONLY COME OUT AT NIGHT, THEN INVESTIGATING THEM IS PARTICULARLY TRICKY. ONLY GO OUT WITH A RESPONSIBLE ADULT AFTER DARK... ONE THAT YOU ARE CERTAIN ISN'T A VAMPIRE!

LOOK OUT FOR ANYONE YOU KNOW THAT IS VERY PALE AND BURNS VERY EASILY IN THE SUN. COULD THEY BE A VAMPIRE?

Other people believe that vampires don't go out during the day because the sunlight would kill them. Have you ever seen a movie where a vampire bursts into flames as soon as it sets foot outside in the sun? What if this is true in real life as well?

Do More Vampires Come out at Night?

Vampires are very private and very clever, so you're extremely unlikely to stumble upon one out in the wild, let alone a whole **COVEN** wandering down your street. It's a far better idea to single out someone that you already **SUSPECT** could be a vampire and track their movements very closely. If you know where this person lives, then it will make your investigation far easier. If you're lucky enough, you may even be able to spy one from the comfort of your own bedroom!

You will need:
- Clock
- Notepad
- Pen or pencil

Method:

1. During the day, while it's still light outside, head to a **LOCATION** where you think a vampire lives. If you're lucky enough, this might be on your street. If not, maybe it's somewhere a bit spookier, like a graveyard... but make sure it's safe.

2. Get settled somewhere safe and comfortable that gives you a good view.

3. Stay there for a set amount of time – try half an hour – and count how many people you see walk past.

4. Now go back after the sun has gone down. Stay there for half an hour and count how many people walk past. Compare the numbers – which is higher? Did you spot your vampire suspect?

21.30

Remember to keep track of all your variables:
Independent variable (the thing you change): time of day
Dependent variable (the thing you measure): number of people (or vampires!)
Control variable (the thing you keep the same): location

So, did you learn anything interesting from your experiment? Did more people seem to come out at night or during the day? Was there anything SUSPICIOUS about these people that made you think they were vampires, or could it have just been your neighbor taking their dog for a late walk? If you're not sure about how reliable your results are, you can always repeat your experiment over a few more nights. You can then find the mode, median, mean, and range for your results.

Case Study: Vlad the Impaler

As scary as these monsters are, there are some real-life people who could scare even a vampire to death. Vlad III, or Vlad the Impaler, was the ruler of a **REGION** called Wallachia in what is now Romania in the mid-15th century. He was born in around 1431 in Transylvania, an area of Romania that is well-known for being a vampire hot spot.

VAMPIRE INVESTIGATORS AND VAMPIRE HUNTERS FROM ACROSS THE WORLD TRAVEL TO TRANSYLVANIA IN THE HOPES OF CATCHING A GLIMPSE OF THE MONSTERS.

VLAD THE IMPALER

Vlad III was a cruel and **RUTHLESS** ruler. He got his nickname, Vlad the Impaler, from the gruesome ways he would **TORTURE** people. After capturing his enemies, they would be stuck through their chests with a large **STAKE** and then stuck into the ground, and left to die. This is called impalement. Vlad used his impaled victims to scare away invaders. During one battle in 1462, Vlad left a horrible surprise for his enemies, the Ottomans. Historians believe that Vlad and his army filled a field with over 20,000 impaled bodies. After seeing this, the Ottomans turned around and ran from the battle in fear.

Vlad III was mean, cruel, and bloodthirsty, but he was no vampire. However, he does have a few things in common with a very famous **FICTIONAL** one... the famous vampire Count Dracula is not only said to live in the same region that Vlad III was born in, they also share a name!

BRAM STOKER'S BOOK, *DRACULA*, WAS ABOUT A VAMPIRE. SOME PEOPLE THINK THAT THE VAMPIRE WAS NAMED AFTER VLAD III. WAS HE **INSPIRED** BY THE STORIES OF VLAD DRACULA?

Vlad III's father was known as Vlad II, or Vlad Dracul. Vlad II was part of a special group called the Order of the Dragon, which is where he got the second part of his name from. "Draco" means "dragon" in an old language called Latin. Vlad III is sometimes known as Vlad Dracula, which means "son of Dracul," or "son of the dragon." However, "dracula" has come to have another meaning... devil. Could this have been what Count Dracula's creator, Bram Stoker, had in mind when he named his character?

Investigation 2: Human Blood?

Vampires are known for their pale skin, red eyes, and sharp fangs. These sharp fangs are very important to a vampire because they are said to use them to pierce the skin of their victims in order to get to their blood. Have you ever seen two red dots on the side of someone's neck? Maybe you've seen these in a scary movie or a book about vampires, or maybe even in real life?

Some vampire investigators believe that when a person is bitten by a vampire, they become a vampire, too! Other investigators disagree and believe that a person only becomes a vampire when they are cursed or drink the blood of a vampire.

Although many people believe that vampires could survive on just raw meat and animal blood if they really needed to, it's said that they much prefer the taste of human blood. If vampires really are out there, and you happen to come across a very hungry one, then you could be in serious danger. It's always best to be safe, so whenever you're on a mission or carrying out an investigation, make sure that your neck is covered. Whether you believe that there are vampires out there or not, you can never be too careful!

A thirsty vampire is said to be unstoppable, so there's no chance of fighting one off. If you come across one in the middle of one of your investigations, it is best to abandon the experiment and quickly get to safety.

VAMPIRE FANGS ARE VERY EASY TO SPOT. THEY'RE MUCH LONGER AND SHARPER THAN HUMAN TEETH.

What Do Vampires Like to Drink?

Do you think there could be a vampire living in your house? Now that you know what they're said to drink, you should also know how to tempt them out. If someone in your family really is a vampire, then this experiment should lead you straight to them in no time.

DO YOU THINK ANY THIRSTY VAMPIRES WILL COME ACROSS YOUR "HUMAN BLOOD"? MAKE A PREDICTION OF WHAT YOU THINK WILL HAPPEN AND COMPARE IT TO YOUR RESULTS ONCE YOU HAVE FINISHED.

You will need:
- Measuring jug
- Two cups
- Red juice
- Timer
- Pen or pencil
- Paper
- Notepad

Method:

1. Measure out some red juice, like black currant or cherry, and pour it into a cup. Leave it out somewhere safe where people will see it.

2. Leave the cup of juice out for three hours. Remember to keep checking your timer so that you don't run over!

3. Check back after three hours and see whether anyone has taken a sip. Pour what is left into the measuring jug to see how much has been drunk.

4. Now, repeat your experiment, but this time leave a sign out with your juice that reads: "Human Blood!" If there are any vampires living in your house, they're sure to believe it and fall for your trick!

5. Leave your cup of "human blood" out for three hours and check back to see if anyone has had any. Pour this into your measuring jug to see how much is left.

6. Write down all of your observations so that you can read over them later.

Remember to keep track of all your variables:

Independent variable (the thing you change): whether the cup is filled with juice or "blood" (whether you leave a sign out or not)

Dependent variable (the thing you measure): how much juice, or "blood," has been drunk

Control variables (the things you keep the same): location, amount of juice or "blood"

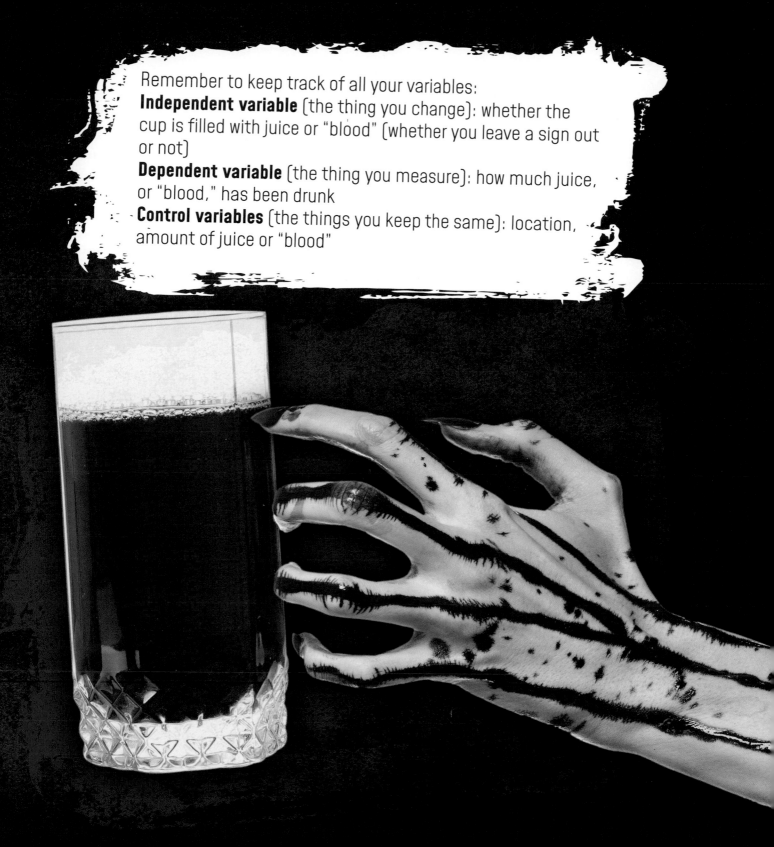

What do your results seem to tell you? Were any vampires tempted by your cup of "blood," or was it left untouched? Did more people seem interested in the cup of juice than the cup of "blood"? Maybe they were both drunk completely, or perhaps they were both still full at the end of your investigation. Even if your investigation didn't go how you predicted, there could still be some useful information that you could gather from your results.

Case Study: Dracula

In 1897, the author Bram Stoker created one of the most terrifying monsters the world has ever known. In the book *Dracula*, Count Dracula is an evil vampire from Transylvania who travels to England in search of his next victims. He is smart, dangerous, and difficult to catch. He can transform himself into a bat, wolf, rat, and even mist.

BRAM STOKER

SOME PEOPLE HAVE SUGGESTED THAT BRAN CASTLE IN ROMANIA IS THE REAL-LIFE CASTLE DRACULA.

In Stoker's book, Dracula lives in a castle hidden away in the Carpathian Mountains in Transylvania. Could this castle really exist? Many vampire investigators believe that Dracula could have existed in real life many years ago, and isn't just a character from a scary book. Some have even traveled to Transylvania in the hopes of tracking down his castle.

Professor Abraham Van Helsing is a vampire hunter in *Dracula* who made it his mission to find and destroy Count Dracula. Although Dracula doesn't make it easy for Van Helsing and his crew, they are eventually successful in destroying the vampire for good. But how did they do it?

According to many vampire investigators and vampire hunters, the only way to really destroy a vampire is by stabbing it through its heart before cutting its head off. Although the characters in *Dracula* used a knife to stab Count Dracula, a wooden stake is said to work very well, too.

WOODEN STAKE

Going up to people and stabbing them through the heart is never a good idea. What if that "vampire" is really just someone who enjoys wearing black clothes and listening to rock music? It's far safer for you, and for everyone else, if you learn how to **REPEL** vampires instead of learning how to kill them.

Investigation 3: Garlic

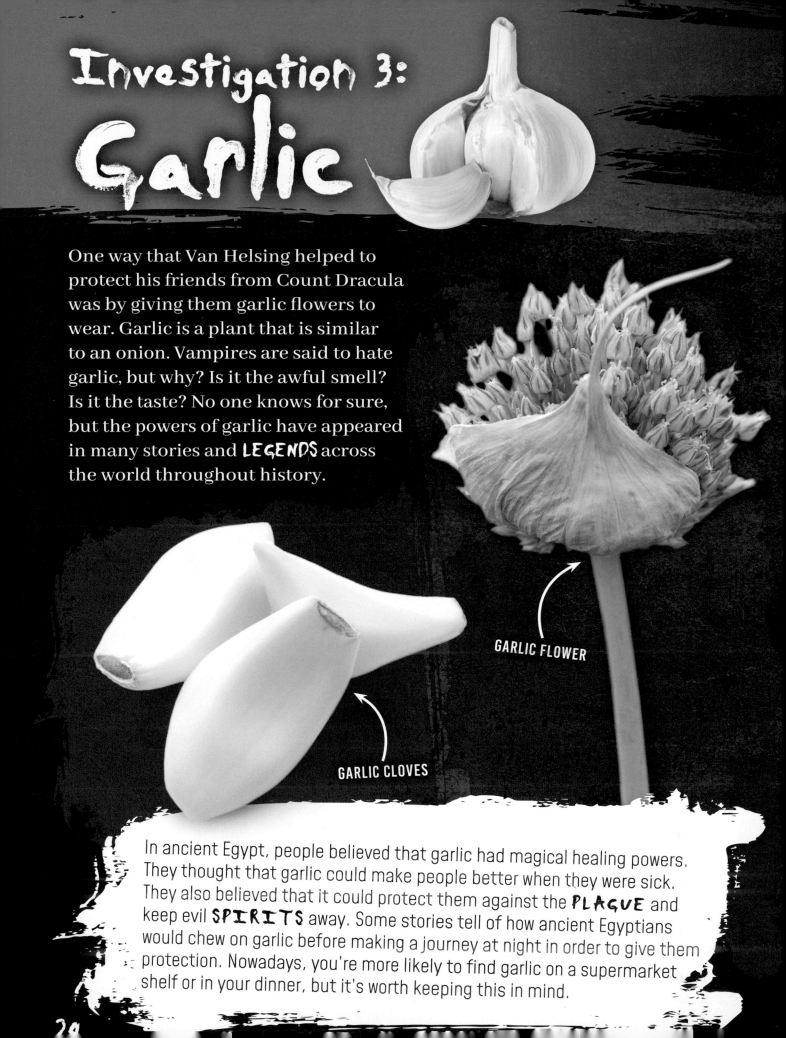

One way that Van Helsing helped to protect his friends from Count Dracula was by giving them garlic flowers to wear. Garlic is a plant that is similar to an onion. Vampires are said to hate garlic, but why? Is it the awful smell? Is it the taste? No one knows for sure, but the powers of garlic have appeared in many stories and **LEGENDS** across the world throughout history.

GARLIC FLOWER

GARLIC CLOVES

In ancient Egypt, people believed that garlic had magical healing powers. They thought that garlic could make people better when they were sick. They also believed that it could protect them against the **PLAGUE** and keep evil **SPIRITS** away. Some stories tell of how ancient Egyptians would chew on garlic before making a journey at night in order to give them protection. Nowadays, you're more likely to find garlic on a supermarket shelf or in your dinner, but it's worth keeping this in mind.

In *Dracula*, no vampires can get anywhere near the vampire hunters while they are protected by the garlic flowers. If you think there could be a vampire living in your town, it might be a good idea to keep some garlic cloves or garlic flowers in your pocket. Even if you don't suspect that there is a vampire nearby, or you're not sure about how **EFFECTIVE** garlic is against vampires, it's always better to be safe than sorry.

The only way to know whether this could work in real life or not is by carrying out a scientific investigation. How could you test this out? Is there any way you could trick someone into eating some garlic and watching for their reaction? Or could you perhaps try hanging some garlic bulbs up around your house and seeing whether anyone stops coming around to visit?

How Much Do Vampires Hate Garlic?

So, you think there could be a vampire living in your house? Perhaps it's your mom, your dad, your brother, your sister, or maybe even your grandma. No matter who it is, you'll need to carry out an investigation to know for certain. To see if vampires hate garlic as much as they do in the stories, try secretly adding some to your suspected vampire's food and see how they react.

You will need:
- One suspected vampire
- Several plates of food
- A small spoon
- Garlic
- Notepad
- Pen or pencil

Method:

1. Seek out the person that you think could be a vampire and keep a close eye on them.

2. On the first day of your investigation, secretly add a small amount of garlic to your suspected vampire's dinner. Try one-quarter of a teaspoon at first.

3. Add the same amount of garlic to another family member's dinner. They will be your control and you can compare their reaction with your suspected vampire's. Who stops eating their dinner first?

4. Record how much of the meal both people eat.

5. On the next day, add a little bit more garlic to both plates again. Try half a teaspoon this time.

6. Again, record how much they both eat.

7. Repeat these steps for a week or until the suspected vampire can't eat any of their meal.

8. Write down all of your findings so that you can analyze them later.

Remember to keep track of all your variables:

Independent variable (the thing you change): amount of garlic

Dependent variable (the thing you measure): how much food is eaten by the suspected vampire

Control variable (the thing you keep the same): type of food and amount of garlic given to suspected vampire and control family member

WHAT DO YOU PREDICT WILL HAPPEN? COMPARE YOUR ACTUAL FINDINGS WITH YOUR PREDICTION WHEN YOU FINISH YOUR EXPERIMENT.

Did you find out anything interesting from your investigation? Did your experiment teach you anything new about vampires, or did your results come out exactly as you expected? You will need to compare your results with your prediction very carefully. If your results seem a bit strange or unexpected, it can sometimes be a good idea to repeat your experiment a few times. You can then compare the results you get from all your repeated experiments. This will make your investigation far more reliable!

Case Study: Vampire Bats

The vampire bat is a type of bat that drinks the blood of other animals to survive. Vampire bats are found across the Americas and usually feed on cows, pigs, chickens, and birds, as well as other forest animals. They sleep in hollow trees and caves during the day and come out at night in search of their prey. Once they have found their next meal, they use their sharp teeth to make a small cut in an animal's skin before licking up the blood that flows from it.

Some vampire bats carry a disease called rabies, and they can pass it on to the animals that they feed off. Rabies is very dangerous, and both animals and humans can catch it. It can be months before any SYMPTOMS appear. Some of these symptoms in humans include a high temperature, a headache, finding it difficult to swallow, and not being able to move.

VAMPIRE BATS HAVE SHARP, POINTY CANINE TEETH, JUST LIKE THE VAMPIRES YOU'RE ALREADY FAMILIAR WITH.

It's very rare for vampire bats to bite humans, so there's very little risk of catching rabies from one. However, in 2017, there was a sudden and unexpected OUTBREAK that saw several attacks on people in Brazil. Around 40 people were bitten by vampire bats, and many of the attacks took place while people were asleep in their beds. Some people even caught rabies. Before this, people didn't believe that vampire bats fed off human blood, but we now know that it is possible.

But what made these bats so hungry for human blood? Some scientists think that these particular bats were very hungry and were struggling to find any of the animals that they would usually feed from, which led them to humans. However, some vampire investigators disagree with this. They believe that vampires have the power to transform themselves into bats and that this could explain why these vampire bats chose to drink human blood. Could these bats really have been vampires in disguise?

Debrief

Well done, investigator. You've carried out many investigations and experiments, and hopefully you've learned a lot about vampires along the way, too. You may have come to the end of this book, but your time as a vampire investigator has just begun. From Count Dracula of Transylvania to the vampire bats of the Americas, there's always more to study and explore. Whether you think there's a vampire living in your town, or you want to read more about Vlad the Impaler, you should have plenty of ideas to get you started on your journey.

It's not easy being a vampire investigator. You'll meet many **SKEPTICS**. Whether you believe that vampires are real or not, it's your job to investigate the mystery and collect any evidence that could be out there.

Glossary

allergic	when a person has a condition that causes their body to have an unusual reaction to certain things
canine	long, sharp tooth in the top of the mouth
centuries	periods of one hundred years
coven	a group of individuals, usually used for witches with similar interests or ideas
effective	able to make happen or change something
fictional	something that is made up and not real
identified	spotted or recognized
inspired	influenced or caused to happen
intelligent	clever or smart
leads	hints or clues
legends	stories from a long time ago that have been passed down
location	the exact position or place of something or someone
nocturnal	active at night instead of during the day
outbreak	a sudden increase in activity of something unwelcome or unpleasant, such as disease
plague	a deadly disease
prey	to hunt, catch, and eat another animal or person
region	a large space or area
repel	to ward off or push away
ruthless	having no sympathy; cruel
skeptics	nonbelievers; people who question or doubt the beliefs that are accepted by other people
spirits	beings that are not part of this world, such as a ghost or devil
stake	a sharpened, pointed wooden post
suspect	believed to be true
suspicious	lacking trust
symptoms	things that happen in the body suggesting that there is a disease or disorder
torture	to deliberately cause great pain to a person or animal
transparent	see-through
victims	people who are harmed as the result of crime

Index